Ripley's Believe It or Not!

WEIRD-ITIES!

PUBLISHING

Publisher Anne Marshall

Editorial Director Rebecca Miles

Assistant Editor Charlotte Howell

Text Geoff Tibballs

Proofreader Judy Barratt

Picture Researchers James Proud, Charlotte Howell

Art Director Sam South

Senior Designer Michelle Foster

Reprographics Juice Creative

Executive Vice President Norm Deska

Vice President, Archives and Exhibits Edward Meyer

PUBLISHER'S NOTE

While every effort has been made to verify the accuracy of the entries in this book, the Publishers cannot be held responsible for any errors contained in the work. They would be glad to receive any information from readers.

WARNING

Some of the stunts and activities in this book are undertaken by experts and should not be attempted by anyone without adequate training and supervision.

Published by Ripley Publishing 2013

Ripley Publishing, Suite 188, 7576 Kingspointe Parkway, Orlando, Florida 32819, USA

2 4 6 8 10 9 7 5 3 1

ISBN 978-1-60991-020-4

Some of this material first appeared in *Ripley's Believe It or Not! Expect... The Unexpected*

Library of Congress Cataloging-in-Publication data is available

Manufactured in China in February/2013 by Leo Paper 1st printing

Ripley's Believe It or Not!

WEIRD-ITIES!

SIMPLY UNBELIEVABLE

RIPLEY
PUBLISHING

a Jim Pattison Company

SIMPLY UNBELIEVABLE

Strange but true. Just when you thought you had seen everything... Find out about the Chinese man who uses his tongue and fingers to paint, the man who set himself up as a human dartboard, and the astonishing two-headed peacock.

PAGE 17

PAGE 22

SOUNDS CRAZY

If Ken Butler's collection of musical instruments doesn't strike a chord with some listeners, it's hardly surprising. Ken dismisses conventional instruments in favor of the toothbrush violin, the golf-club sitar, or the hockey-stick cello.

New Yorker Ken created his first hybrid instrument in 1978 by adding a fingerboard, tailpiece, tuning pegs, and a bridge to a small hatchet, which he then played as a violin. The success of his ax violin led him to create more than 200 additional wacky instruments from such diverse objects as bicycle wheels, umbrellas, shotguns, and snow shovels. He usually chooses objects that are of roughly similar shape or proportion to the instrument that they then become.

The American musician and visual artist, who studied the viola as a child, has seen his creations displayed in museums and galleries in Peru, Europe, and Tokyo, as well as in several Ripley's museums. In 1997, he released an album—Voices of Anxious Objects—and he has performed with ensembles playing 15 of his instruments.

Musician Ken Butler, surrounded by some of his wacky instruments, including a hockey-stick cello in the top row.

To decide what would make a good instrument, Ken Butler seeks out objects that are relatively strong, but also relatively lightweight, and that allow for the placement of tuning pegs and strings.

LONG-LIFE BREAD

Vivien Anderson from Cambridgeshire, England, holds a bread roll that dates from World War I! It was given to her grandfather in a ration pack while he was serving in the conflict. Handed down through the family, the roll is estimated to be about 90 years old.

STRONG BOY

When Rique Schill, from Jamestown, North Dakota, was pinned under the family Ford in 1984, his nine-year-old son Jeremy lifted the 4,000-lb (1,814-kg) car despite the fact that he weighed only 65 lb (30 kg) himself.

CAUGHT ON CAMERA

Michael Adams, from Manchester, England, chose an unwise target for a robbery—a shop specializing in security cameras. His raid was caught on eight different CCTV cameras!

CAR PLUNGE

In 2004, a car containing four teenage girls plunged over a 108-ft (33-m) cliff in Britain and flipped over three times before landing upright on rocks just a few feet from the swell of a raging sea. Incredibly, the girls' worst injury was a broken ankle.

STATIC SPARK

In 2002, Bob Clewis, 52, of San Antonio, Texas, survived a gas-station explosion after a simple spark of static electricity from his jacket ignited and engulfed him in flames.

ICE FALL

Although it was a warm summer's day, a cricket match near Faversham, England, was interrupted in 2005 when a huge chunk of ice fell from the sky and exploded onto the field. At the time, the sky was cloud-free and there were no aircraft in sight.

PERFECT PRESENT

Helen Swisshelm received the best Christmas present in 2001—a class ring that she had lost 53 years earlier! She last saw the gold-and-onyx ring in 1948 while swimming with friends in the Hudson River near her home in Cohoes, New York. She gave up hope of ever seeing it again until, more than half a century later, she received a call at her home in Lutz, Florida, from a nun at the Catholic school she had attended in Albany. A man with a metal detector scouring the Hudson had found a 1948 class ring bearing the school's shield and, via initials on the ring, the nuns matched the year and letters to Mrs. Swisshelm.

BULLET SURPRISE

After waking up with a headache, swollen lips, and powder burns in June 2005, Wendell Coleman, 47, of Jacksonville, Florida, went to hospital, where doctors found a bullet embedded in his tongue. Coleman didn't even know he'd been shot.

HOUSE SPARED

A houseowner in California must be the luckiest in the world. When the fires that devastated 663,000 acres (268,300 ha) of southern

California in 2003 reached the wealthy suburb of Scripps Ranch, 16 mi (26 km) from San Diego, flames destroyed every house in the street except one.

SMOKING NEST

Fire chief Donald Konkle, of Harrisburg, Pennsylvania, decided that a house fire had been started when a bird picked up a smoldering cigarette while building its nest!

HIGH AND DRY

A seal was left high and dry when he found himself stranded on top of a post off the coast of Scotland. He had to wait nine hours before the tide came in sufficiently for him to roll back into the water.

TWO LAURAS

In June 2001, when Laura Buxton, from Staffordshire, England, released a balloon at her tenth birthday party, it traveled 140 mi (225 km) before being found in Wiltshire, England, by another ten-year-old girl, Laura Buxton! Not only did the girls share the same name and age, but they discovered they also had the same hair color and owned the same kinds of pet—a dog, a guinea pig, and a rabbit.

MISSING PEN

In 1953, Boone Aiken lost his engraved fountain pen in Florence, South Carolina. Three years later, while in New York City, Mrs. Aiken spotted a pen on the street next to their hotel. It was the lost one.

WALLET RECOVERED

When James Lubeck's wallet slipped from his pocket into Marblehead Harbor, Massachusetts, in 1966, he never expected to see it again. But in August 2005, he heard from Antonio Randazzo, who had hauled in the wallet's collection of credit cards in a netful of cod, flounder, and haddock 25 mi (40 km) away from where Lubeck had lost it.

SAME BIRTHDAY

Four generations of one family from Brisbane, Australia, share the same birthday—August 1. Norma Steindl was born on August 1, 1915; her son Leigh on August 1, 1945; Leigh's daughter Suzanna on, August 1, 1973; and Suzanna's son Emmanuel on August 1, 2003.

CHRISTMAS CHEER

When Matilda Close was born on Christmas Day 2003, in Victoria, Australia, believe it or not, she was the third generation of her family to be born on December 25! Her mother Angela and her grandmother, Jean Carr, were both born on Christmas Day.

HEART-STOPPER

While remodeling his bathroom in 2005, Nigel Kirk, from Burton-on-Trent, England, came within 0.04 in (1 mm) of dying after accidentally shooting himself in the heart with a nail gun. As he worked, 53-year-old Nigel slipped and managed to fire a 2-in (5-cm) steel tack straight into his heart. Luckily, the tack hit hard scar-tissue that had built up from an illness he had suffered 30 years earlier and just missed his vital heart vessels.

CHEWING CHALK

Rena Bronson, of Macon, Georgia, has a weird food craving—she eats chalk every day! She has been devouring chunks of the white clay called kaolin since 1992. Although it has made her constipated, she says that she likes the creamy consistency in her mouth.

DESERT ORDEAL

Max, a one-year-old golden retriever, survived after spending 3 weeks and 3 days stranded in the Arizona desert in 2005. Max ran off after his owner Mike Battles's truck was involved in a road accident. The dog was eventually found lying under a bush.

DOUBLE BIRTH

Twins Mary Maurer and Melanie Glavich gave birth to sons 35 minutes apart in 2005. They had the same due date, May 27, but both sisters went into labor early. They delivered in adjoining rooms at the same hospital in Middleburg Heights, Ohio.

LONG-LOST SOLDIERS

When Harry Dillon, sent out a letter addressed with nothing but a former comrade's name and a guessed city, the British ex-soldiers were reunited after 50 years!

LONG OVERDUE

A book was returned to a Californian library in 2005—78 years late! Jim Pavon said he discovered the copy of Rudyard Kipling's *Kim* in a box belonging to his late aunt, who had borrowed it from a library in Oakland in 1927. The library waived the fine of around $600 that had accrued on the overdue book.

HOLDING ON

Skydiver and sky-surfer, Greg Gasson regularly performs amazing stunts in the air. Here he hangs precariously over Eloy, Arizona, holding on by only one strap of his parachute, thousands of feet above the ground.

TYING THE KNOT

Boonthawee Seangwong and Kanjana Kaetkeow tied the knot on Valentine's Day (February 14) 2006, at Pattaya beach resort in Thailand.

The highlight of the Thai wedding, complete with chanting monks, centipedes, and scorpions, was that the "wedding room" took the shape of a coffin. The bride's 32 days spent in a plastic cage with 3,400 scorpions in 2002 can only be matched by the groom's 28 days in a cage with 1,000 centipedes in 2003.

INSECT INVASION

In November 2004, tourists holidaying in the Canary Islands, which lie off the northwest coast of Africa, received a shock when they were joined on the beach by a swarm of approximately 100 million pink locusts. Many of the migrating insects didn't live long enough to enjoy the scenery, however, having suffered broken legs and battered wings while crossing the sea in high winds and heavy rain.

UNWANTED GIFTS

Horst Lukas, of Iserlohn, Germany, was sent 12 bicycles, four boats, a mobile home, and dozens of tickets for rock concerts after a hacker spent $500,000 on eBay using his name.

FRUIT FIGHT

Every year, villagers at Ivrea in northern Italy re-enact a medieval battle by dressing up as soldiers and pelting each other with oranges!

BENDY BODIES

Contortionists with the State Circus of Mongolia perform extraordinary feats by bending their bodies into seemingly excrutiating shapes. Their limbs and joints are so flexible that they are able to bend into extreme positions.

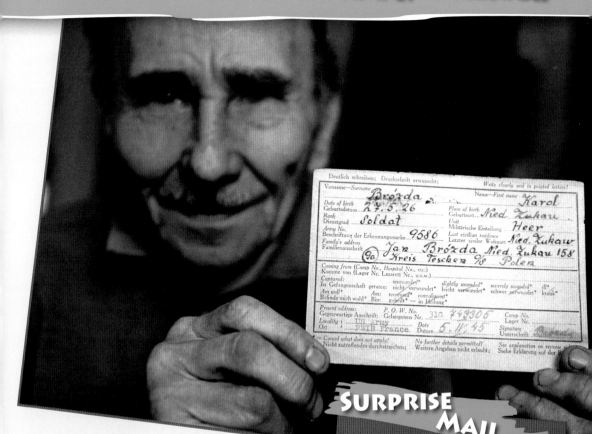

SURPRISE MAIL

Former Polish soldier Karol Brozda, 79, now living in the Czech Republic, holds up a letter he sent to his parents from a U.S. prison camp in France in February 1945, assuring them that he was alive. His parents received the letter in March 2005!

CROC ATTACK

Shelly Hazlett has had 29 operations since being savaged by a huge crocodile during a show at her uncle's croc park in Australia. When Shelly slipped in mud, the reptile clamped its jaws on her lower torso and let go only when her father gouged out its eyes.

MAGNETIC POWER

Erika zur Stimberg is irresistible—to forks, spoons, and frying pans, which for the past 12 years have been flying toward her and sticking to her body. Doctors, in Brakel, Germany, are at a loss to explain her magnetism.

FALSE (TEETH) ALARM

Three years after losing his dentures in a fall, a Taiwanese man discovered in 2005 that they had been stuck in one of his bronchial tubes all the time. The 45-year-old sought medical attention when he started to have breathing difficulties. This lead to the amazing discovery of the missing dentures.

EXTRA FINGERS

Devender Harne, an 11-year-old boy from Nagpur, India, has a total of 25 fingers and toes. The five extra digits are functional and normal in size and do not prevent Devender playing his favorite sport of cricket.

NOT STRICTLY BALLROOM

MS DanceR is a robotic dance partner that has been manufactured in Japan. The robot's memory holds the waltz pattern, predicting the next step of the dance and following a human lead, but it can also sense pressure in its arms and back in order to stay in sync with its human partner.

FAVORITE DRINK

A family in Cheshire, England, are so addicted to the fruit-cordial drink Vimto that they have a subterranean tank of the stuff in the garden. Pipes carry the liquid from the tank to the kitchen, where it is available on tap.

SHRIMP SHOWER

It rained shrimp on Mount Soledad, California, in April 2005. Hundreds of the tiny crustacea fell from the sky during a storm. Experts said that juvenile shrimp frequently gather together in large numbers in shallow water during rough weather out at sea and that they had probably been carried inland by a sea spout.

ANGEL CAMERA

Laurie Robinson is no ordinary photographer. She likes to take pictures of tombstones in cemeteries in Los Angeles,

ALL BUTTONED UP

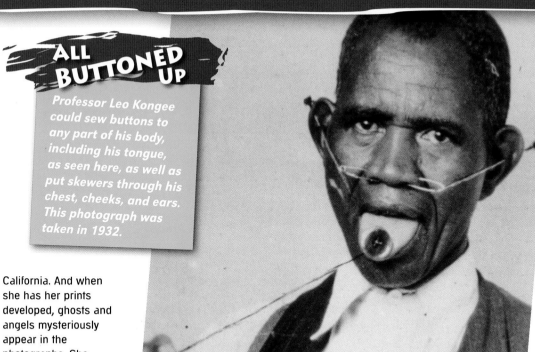

Professor Leo Kongee could sew buttons to any part of his body, including his tongue, as seen here, as well as put skewers through his chest, cheeks, and ears. This photograph was taken in 1932.

California. And when she has her prints developed, ghosts and angels mysteriously appear in the photographs. She believes that the spirits show up in her pictures because of the positive energy she sends out.

LION GUARD

Believe it or not, a 12-year-old Ethiopian girl owes her safety to a pack of lions. The girl was abducted in June 2005 by seven men who wanted to force her into marriage, but the kidnappers were chased away by three lions that amazingly then stood guard over the girl for at least half a day. A police sergeant said: "They stood guard until we found her and then they just left her like a gift and went back into the forest. Everyone thinks this is some kind of miracle." A wildlife expert suggested that the girl's crying might have been mistaken for the mewing sound of a cub, which would explain why the lions didn't eat her.

SHOCKING EXPERIENCE

A man built up at least 30,000 volts of static electricity in his jacket simply by walking around the Australian city of Warrnambool, Victoria, in September 2005. Frank Clewer left a trail of scorch marks, carpet burns, and molten plastic behind him.

CRUSHING BLOW

Two men escaped from a Kentucky jail in 2005 and hid in a garbage truck— only for their bodies to be discovered in a nearby landfill the following day. The jailbirds hadn't realized that, to prevent exactly this kind of escape, the prison requires that all garbage be compacted twice before it leaves the grounds.

NAILED IT

Experiencing toothache and blurry vision, Patrick Lawler, of Denver, Colorado, went to a dentist in January 2005, only to learn that he had shot a 4-in (10-cm) nail through his mouth into his skull with a nail gun!

HEADLESS FOWL

On September 10, 1945, farmer Lloyd Olsen chopped off 5½-month-old Mike's head with an ax in readiness for the cooking pot, but the headless rooster continued pecking for food around the farm at Fruita, Colorado!

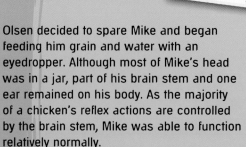

Olsen visited Los Angeles, San Diego, Atlantic City, and New York working the sideshows with his "Wonder Chicken" Mike.

Olsen decided to spare Mike and began feeding him grain and water with an eyedropper. Although most of Mike's head was in a jar, part of his brain stem and one ear remained on his body. As the majority of a chicken's reflex actions are controlled by the brain stem, Mike was able to function relatively normally.

Over the next 18 months, the chicken's weight increased from 2½ lb (1.1 kg) to 8 lb (3.6 kg) and, insured for $10,000, Mike toured the U.S.A. as the "Wonder Chicken," with Lloyd charging 25 cents for a peek. Finally, he choked on his way back from an appearance in Arizona. Olsen was unable to find the eyedropper used to clear Mike's open esophagus and Mike died.

Mike the Headless Chicken would "peck" for food and "preen" his feathers, just like the other chickens on the farm.

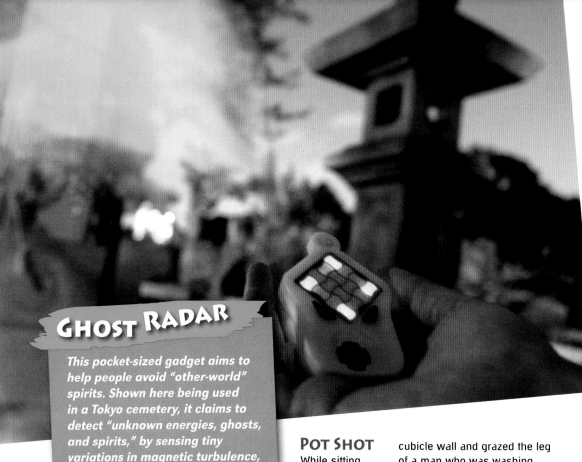

GHOST RADAR

This pocket-sized gadget aims to help people avoid "other-world" spirits. Shown here being used in a Tokyo cemetery, it claims to detect "unknown energies, ghosts, and spirits," by sensing tiny variations in magnetic turbulence, light, and temperature, and then giving position and movement. Instructions contain details on eight types of specter that range from harmless lost souls stuck in this world to evil spirits.

HAPPY ACCIDENT

Eddie May Jr., of Georgia, choked on a piece of food while driving, blacked out, then hit a passing car. The impact knocked the food from his throat and he awoke uninjured!

POT SHOT

While sitting on the toilet in April 2005, an off-duty Texan police officer accidentally shot a man. Officer Craig Clancy was answering a call of nature in San Antonio when his gun fell from its holster as he pulled down his pants. In trying to catch the gun, he grabbed the trigger and fired two bullets, one of which went through the cubicle wall and grazed the leg of a man who was washing his hands at the time.

INCRIMINATING EVIDENCE

After ordering a pizza and asking for a job application form, a man suddenly produced a gun and robbed a Las Vegas pizza parlor of $200 in June 2005. But police didn't have to do much detective work to catch him. He left behind the partially completed form, which included his name and address.

DOZED OFF

A cargo plane circled for more than half an hour in March 2005 because an air-traffic controller at Nice Airport, France, had fallen asleep.

OLD NEIGHBOR

Gilbert Fogg, of Nettleham, England, discovered that his neighbor Tom Parker was actually a long-lost comrade from World War II, whom he thought had died in battle!

BAIL BLUNDER

After being arrested for possession of counterfeit money in 2005, fraudster Darrell Jenkins, from Springfield, Massachusetts, tried to pay his $500 bail using fake notes!

DOG'S DINNER

A man from Schaarbeek, Belgium, set his apartment on fire in April 2005 after trying to cremate his pet dog on a barbecue and using far too much gasoline!

TEA THIEF

A man who stole a tractor-trailer truck in Washington State in 2005 had to call 911 for medical help after drinking from a cup he found in the cab. What he thought was a refreshing drink was in fact the truck driver's tobacco spit!

KING OF CUBES

Believe it or not, 14-year-old Shotaro Makisumi, from Japan, can solve a "3 x 3 x 3" Rubik's cube puzzle in a mere 13.72 seconds.

THE GREAT ESCAPE

The Dark Master of Escape, Canadian Steve Santini, also known as "The World's Most Extreme Escape Artist," puts the fear back into escapology with his blend of heavy metal and medieval torture.

How did you become interested in escapology?
"I did a book report for school on Houdini, and then started to experiment on my own. There were no instruction books—my parents kept getting calls: 'Your kid's jumping into our pool wrapped in bike chains.'"

How did it develop?
"I broke out of my first jail cell at a police station when I was 14 (I was put in there voluntarily!). I used to buy up old cuffs and locks, rip them apart, and see how they worked. I didn't know trick locks existed—I just learned how to defeat normal mechanisms."

Have you ever feared for your life during a stunt?
"On New Year's Eve 2005, when I performed the Cremation Chamber. It was watched by an audience of 35,000 people and 15 million live on television—the most ever to witness a single escape. I was in a vault with walls just one-eighth of an inch thick, and I was handcuffed and padlocked to a chain welded inside the door. On three sides of the vault were propane flame throwers—I was supposed to be out within one minute, when the temperature hit 400°F and the air became unbreathable. But one of the cuffs jammed, and I had to hold my breath until I could break free."

What other escapes have you performed?
"Lots—my favorites include escaping from a nailed and padlocked coffin submerged under 30 ft of water, and breaking out of a maximum security cell on Canada's Death Row, which had held the last man to be publicly hanged in that country."

What makes your shows different?
"I got tired of the image of escapologists in glitzy suits in Vegas. I wanted to remove the magic from it—by doing all escapes in full view of the audience. What really grabs people has to involve pain and danger. I use sinister heavy-metal music to play that up."

Why "Dark Master"?
"I came up with that not because I'm Satanic or because I'm portraying an evil person, but because I'm facing devices from people's nightmares, from the darkest periods of human history. I combine modern technology—like being pulled toward a chain saw—with ancient devices, like thumb screws and iron maidens."

Do you use hypnotism or contortionist techniques?
"I'm not a contortionist—I'm not a svelte guy! I use hypnotism techniques to focus. But it basically comes down to extreme stubbornness and an incredibly high pain tolerance."

Do you get nervous beforehand?
"Terribly. Every time I do these things, there's genuinely the chance that something will go horribly wrong. Once you're in, you can't panic though—if you do, you're done."

Are you working on any future projects?
"I want to be stretched on a medieval rack and have that lowered under water. No-one's ever got off a rack, let alone a submerged one. No, I'm not a masochist—I just know what will make people go 'whoa!'."

POTATO RING

Forty years after losing her wedding ring in a potato field, a German farmer's wife found it again while eating—it was inside a potato!

BLACK SPOT

In 1966, Christina Cort narrowly escaped death when a truck smashed into her home in Salvador, Brazil. She was still in the same house 23 years later when another truck crashed through the wall—driven by the same man.

IN THE STARS

Born in 1835, the year of Halley's comet, U.S. writer Mark Twain said that as he had come into the world with the comet, so he would pass with it. The comet returned in 1910 and Twain died that April, aged 74.

NIGHT CAP

Russian Vladimir Rasimov drank so much vodka that he fell asleep between train tracks and didn't wake up even when a 140-ton cargo train passed over him.

LOST DRIVER

In 2002, a train driver delayed hundreds of passengers for more than an hour, near Birmingham, England, after admitting he didn't know the route.

PERILOUS PUTT

Harold Parris, who has been playing golf regularly for 55 years, made the mistake of teeing off without his glasses in April 2005. Parris managed to land the ball on the back of an alligator while playing a round at the Robber's Row golf course, South Carolina!

SCREEN DAMAGE

When four horses broke out of their field in Hausen, Germany, in April 2003, only three survived. One horse was killed instantly when he raced across the road and was hit by a car, crashing through the windscreen. Miraculously, the 26-year-old driver was unhurt.

SHINING EXAMPLE

The average light bulb lasts no longer than 1,000 hours. But a carbon filament bulb has been burning in the fire department at Livermore, California, for more than 100 years!

Since being installed in 1901, the four-watt bulb has burned through the birth of powered human flight, women being granted the vote, two world wars, space exploration, 19 U.S. presidents, and 25 Olympic Games. Visitors come from as far away as South Africa and Sweden to check out the famous bulb. Engineers attribute its longevity to a combination of low wattage and filament thickness.

Such is the worldwide interest in the Livermore light bulb that it has its own official website, complete with a live webcam that allows browsers to see that it is still burning.

What makes its survival all-the-more remarkable is that before a local reporter uncovered its history in 1972, Livermore firefighters often batted it for good luck as they clung to the side of the departing fire truck. It has also experienced countless near misses from footballs and Frisbees. Now it is treated like a precious stone. As Tim Simpkins, Inspector with the Livermore-Pleasanton Fire Department, says: "I don't want to be on duty when and if it ever goes out."

Appropriately, the town slogan—adopted in the 1920s because of the area's clean air—is "Live Longer in Livermore."

1901	1920	1940	1960	1980	2001
Wright Brothers Flight 1903	Ford Makes Model-T 1908	Television Invented 1927	Nuclear Age Begins 1945	Pres. Kennedy Assassinated 1963	Pres. Nixon Resigns 1974	PC's Sold By IBM 1981	Internet Growth 1993
Flagpole Raised 1906	WW I 1914	Women Get The Vote 1920	WW II 1941	Disneyland Opens 1955	Man Lands On The Moon 1969	Titanic Found 1985	Berlin Wall Falls 1989
Light Bulb Installed 1901	Livermore 1st Rodeo 1918	Stock Market Crashes 1929	Lawrence Livermore Lab 1952	Woodstock & Altamont 1969	Lightbulb Moved 1976	LPFD Formed 1996	Lightbulb Century 2001

As the world's oldest-known working light bulb, when the Livermore Fire Department bulb was moved to its new home in 1976, it was handled with the greatest care. The bulb was granted Code 3 status and transported with truck lights flashing and sirens wailing.

ANIMAL ARTIST

Koopa the turtle, owned by U.S. artist Kira Varszegi, has sold more than 100 pieces of his own artwork. He creates the paintings by covering his underbelly in paint and sliding around on a canvas. The works usually sell for around $135 a piece.

POETIC JUSTICE

After two U.S. thieves stole a checkbook from the home of Mr. and Mrs. David Conner, they went to a bank with a $200 check made out to themselves. The female teller asked them to wait a minute, then called security. The teller was Mrs. David Conner.

HEAVY BREATHING

Three police cars raced to answer an emergency at a house in Lake Parsippany, New Jersey, one night in August 2005, only to be told by the owner that she had been teaching her German shepherd dog to make 911 calls. The 911 operator heard only "heavy breathing."

SHOT BY DOG

Bulgarian hunter Vasil Plovdiv was shot by his own dog in 2005 when he tried to knock a bird out of its mouth with the butt of his rifle. The German pointer refused to drop the quail and instead leaped at Plovdiv, knocking the trigger and peppering his chest with shot.

BRIGHT SPARK

After locking himself out of his still-running car in Glen Burnie, Maryland, in 2005, an 82-year-old man had the idea of stopping the engine by removing all the gasoline. Unfortunately, he used an electric vacuum cleaner to siphon the fuel and, when a spark ignited the vapors, he was taken to hospital with burns.

TIGHT SQUEEZE

Contortionist Hugo Zamoratte— "The Bottle Man"—dislocates nearly every bone in his body and can squeeze into a bottle!

SMITH PARTY

In Vermont, all 57 of the David Smiths listed in the state's phone books got together for a "David Smith Night!"

DRAWBRIDGE DRAMA

A 79-year-old grandmother had an incredible escape in 2005 after she was left dangling 100 ft (30 m) in the air from a drawbridge. Retired teacher Helen Koton was crossing a canal in Hallandale Beach, Florida, when the drawbridge began to rise. She clung on to the railing as the bridge rose to its full height, leaving her hanging in the air, her handbag swinging from her ankle. Drivers alerted the bridge operator, who lowered Helen back to the ground.

THIN MATERIAL

Physicists from Manchester, England, and Chernogolovka, Russia, have managed to create a flat fabric called "Graphene," which is only a single atom thick!

CHURCH AFLOAT

In 2003, the 2,000-sq-ft (185-sq-m) Malagawatch United Church was moved by water and road 20 mi (32 km) to its new home in Highland Village, Iona, Nova Scotia.

BACKWARD HULA

At the age of just ten, Joyce Hart, of New Jersey, could do a backward somersault through two hoops.

HIDDEN BULLET

For 25 years, Adrian Milton, of New York, had a bullet in his skull but didn't know it. He remembered an incident back in 1976 when blood had suddenly spurted from his head, but he always assumed that he'd been hit by debris from a building site. In fact he'd been shot in the head. His secret emerged in 2001 during a routine visit to the doctor.

CASH FLOW

Two motorcyclists lost $20,000 in cash in 2005 when their backpack burst open on a highway near Winchester, England. Although drivers stopped to help, strong winds blew the notes across the road and only a small portion of the money was recovered.

WHAT'S IN A NAME?

Even by the standards of Martha Stewart's colorful career, the U.S. kitchen goddess came up with a moment to remember in September 2005. On her TV show, she gathered no fewer than 164 Martha Stewart namesakes. They included Martha Stewarts who were married to men with equally famous names—a Jimmy and a Rod—and even a bulldog named Martha Stewart.

HEAD SPACE

Karolyne Smith, of Salt Lake City, Utah, offered her forehead for sale on eBay as the site for

a permanent, tattooed advertisement. The winning bid of $10,000 was made by the Golden Palace online casino.

BODY TALK

Believe it or not, an Indian man lived with his mother's corpse for 21 years. Syed Abdul Ghafoor kept the embalmed body of his mother in a glass casket at his home in Siddavata and even consulted the preserved corpse before making important decisions.

FUTURE VISION

One of the most popular crazes in Las Vegas is the "morph booth," where as many as 300 couples a day line up to see what their virtual reality child would look like. The fotomorphosis machine merges you and your partner's images to produce a supposedly accurate simulation of any future offspring. Some couples are reportedly using the machine before deciding whether or not to get married!

TOAD TOXIN

Dogs in Australia's Northern Territory are getting high by licking toxins from the backs of cane toads. Local veterinarian Megan Pickering said that some dogs were becoming addicted to the hallucinogens and she had treated more than 30 that had overdosed on bufo toxin.

TWO-HEADED PEACOCK

This two-headed peacock was raised on a farm in Texas, and lived to be almost two years old. It was taxidermied by Tim Dobbs, of Midland, Texas, in 2003. Ripley has yet to perform DNA testing to determine if the two heads do indeed belong to the same bird.

PICKLED DRAGON

Scientists at Britain's Natural History Museum could hardly believe their eyes in 2003 when confronted with a pale baby dragon, preserved in a jar of formaldehyde.

The dragon had apparently been discovered by David Hart, the grandson of a former museum porter, during a garage clear-out in Oxfordshire.

Accompanying the find were documents suggesting that the dragon had originally been offered to the Natural History Museum in the late 19th century by German scientists, but that the museum had rejected it as a hoax.

While modern scientists began to re-examine the tale, it emerged that the 19th-century museum curators were right— the dragon was a hoax. But, the current story was also a hoax! Hart had invented it in order to promote a novel written by Allistair Mitchell. The dragon had been made for a BBC TV series *Walking With Dinosaurs*.

The dragon was actually built by BBC model makers and turned out to be part of an elaborate publishing hoax.

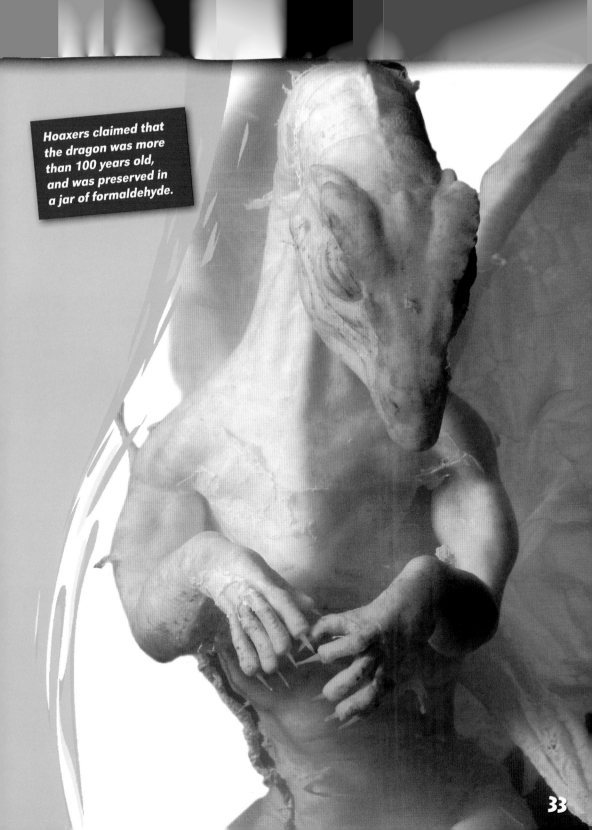

Hoaxers claimed that the dragon was more than 100 years old, and was preserved in a jar of formaldehyde.

TWIN TRAGEDIES

In March 2002, Finnish twin brothers, aged 71, were killed in identical bicycle accidents along the same road, two hours apart. Both men were hit by trucks, the second twin's fatality occurring half a mile from the first's.

YAK-SKIING

Yak-skiing is the new extreme sport that is catching on in Manali, India. A person on skis stands at the foot of a hill holding a bucket of nuts while attached by a long rope fed around a pulley to a yak at the top of the hill. When the bucket is rattled loudly, the yak charges down the hill, yanking the skier up the slope.

IRONIC THEFT

Among items stolen from All Souls Church in Peterborough, England, in July 2005, was a 2-ft (0.6-m) high statue of St. Anthony of Padua, who is the patron saint of lost and stolen items.

DESPERATELY SEEKING...

The Lutheran Church of Landeryd, Sweden, put a "wanted" advertisement in a local newspaper asking for churchgoers.

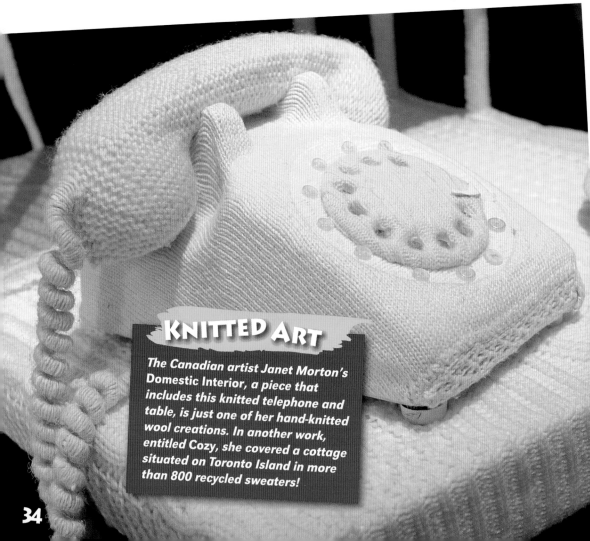

KNITTED ART

The Canadian artist Janet Morton's *Domestic Interior,* a piece that includes this knitted telephone and table, is just one of her hand-knitted wool creations. In another work, entitled *Cozy,* she covered a cottage situated on Toronto Island in more than 800 recycled sweaters!

PLAYING WITH FOOD

The Vienna Vegetable Orchestra is seen here performing in London, England, at a concert that included only vegetables! Formed in 1998, the orchestra consists of musicians playing instruments made almost exclusively of vegetables.

NAME CHECK

On business in Louisville, Kentucky, in the late 1950s, George D. Bryson registered at room 307 at the Brown Hotel. When he jokingly asked if there was any mail for him, the clerk gave him a letter addressed to the previous occupant of the room, another George D. Bryson!

TOTALLY BARKING

Mark Plumb, aged 20, of Houma, Louisiana, was arrested in August 2005 after he allegedly ran barking from a house and bit the local mailman on the shoulder.

SNIFF AND TELL

A German telecommunications company is presently developing the world's first cellular phone that will alert users when their breath is bad!

LUCKY CALL

When stranded in the Andes, Leonard Diaz from Colombia was rescued after a phone company employee called him on his expired cell phone to ask if he wanted to buy more time!

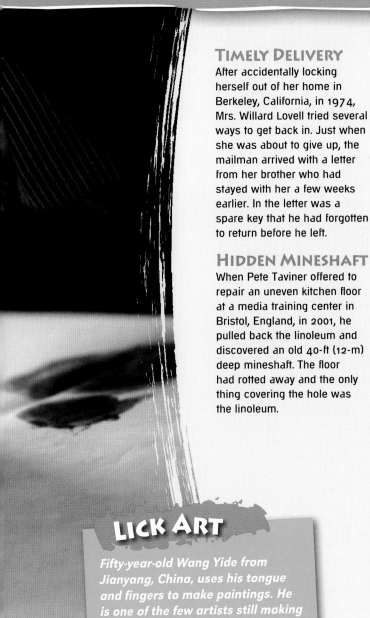

TIMELY DELIVERY

After accidentally locking herself out of her home in Berkeley, California, in 1974, Mrs. Willard Lovell tried several ways to get back in. Just when she was about to give up, the mailman arrived with a letter from her brother who had stayed with her a few weeks earlier. In the letter was a spare key that he had forgotten to return before he left.

HIDDEN MINESHAFT

When Pete Taviner offered to repair an uneven kitchen floor at a media training center in Bristol, England, in 2001, he pulled back the linoleum and discovered an old 40-ft (12-m) deep mineshaft. The floor had rotted away and the only thing covering the hole was the linoleum.

LICK ART

Fifty-year-old Wang Yide from Jianyang, China, uses his tongue and fingers to make paintings. He is one of the few artists still making traditional Chinese paintings using this method.

REGISTERED HAIR-DO

The "comb-over," in which a partially bald person grows hair long on one side and then combs it over the bald spot, is a U.S. patented invention!

PHOTO FIT

Awiey Hernandez was arrested in 2005 when he went to the 90th Precinct station house in Brooklyn, New York, to check on the status of a friend and inadvertently stood directly in front of his own "Wanted" poster!

PIG SAVIOR

Joanne Altsman owes her life to Lulu, her Vietnamese pot-bellied pig. When Joanne suffered a heart attack while on a trailer home holiday on Presque Isle, Pennsylvania, in 1998, Lulu squeezed out of the trailer's dog flap, pushed open the gate and waddled out into the middle of the road where she lay on her back with all four trotters in the air to stop the first passing car. Sure enough, a driver stopped, followed Lulu back into the trailer and found Mrs. Altsman semi-conscious. Doctors later said Joanne would have died within 15 minutes but for the pig's actions. Lulu received a bravery award and a big jam doughnut.

SHOCK FACTOR

The Great Voltini, Welsh electrocution artiste Sebastian Vittorini, loves nothing more than sending half a million volts of electricity through his body until lightning shoots from his fingers.

How did you become interested in electricity?
"I saw a cabaret act with an electric chair and I was fascinated to know how it worked, so I started building one myself. It went from there!"

What is your most famous act?
"The 'Lightning Man' act. I stand or sit on top of a huge Tesla coil—a 14ft-high column of wire named after its inventor Nikola Tesla and made by manufacturer HVFX. It transforms electricity into about half a million high-frequency volts—my body basically becomes a human conductor, and sparks and lightning strands shoot out through my fingertips."

Does it hurt?
"Actually, when you do it right, it's a pleasant kind of tingly feeling. It's only when you do it wrong that it hurts."

What are the dangers involved?
"When you get it wrong, your muscles contract involuntarily, which is very unpleasant—it's the same effect as when a person who has got an electric shock is thrown across the room. It can also cause cardiac arrest—people have died doing this kind of act. Long-term, it can cause partial paralysis owing to long-term nerve damage."

Why do you take the risk?
"So far, I've been shocked only a few times and had minor burns from the sparks. The most frightening thing is that when I'm on the machine, I can't control it myself—so my safety is in someone else's hands. But when I'm doing it, it's amazing. The lightning strands are constantly waving about in front of me. It's the most beautiful thing I've ever seen—I absolutely love it."

Why doesn't the shock kill you instantly?
"It is believed that the frequency is so high—300 kHz as opposed to the 50 Hz of regular household electricity—that the nerves can't sense it, like you can't hear a dog whistle. It would kill me if I was in a complete circuit—if a bolt of lightning connected with something grounded, like a curtain rail, I would die instantly."

Do you do other work with electricity?
"My show features lots of electricity and static stunts—I spend quite a lot of time electrocuting my beautiful assistant Nurse Electra, who is also my girlfriend! I can light a gasoline-soaked torch with the sparks from my hands—I've done that one on national television."

Has it ever got you into trouble?
"In the early days I practiced When I was building my first coil, I got a knock on my door from my next door neighbor—it had destroyed his computer."

What will you do next?
"I'm working on a character called Sir Voltalot for a show loosely based on the Arthurian legends. He will use a huge Tesla coil and electricity to rescue damsels in distress and find the Holy Grail."

AMAZING MEDITATION

In December 2005, Ram Bahadur Bomjon, aged 15, from southern Nepal, claimed to have mastered the art of meditation to such an extent that he had gone without food and water for more than seven months. He plans to meditate for six years to achieve Enlightenment.

2005, he was horrified to find that there were no clovers to be found anywhere in the grounds. Kaminski feared that his great rival, Edward Martin Sr., a retiree of Soldotna, Alaska, would seize the opportunity to expand his own collection of 76,000 four-leaf clovers.

SLICE OF FORTUNE

A slice of singer Justin Timberlake's half-eaten French toast (complete with fork and syrup) sold on eBay for a staggering $4,000.

BANK FOLLY

Thomas E. Mason was charged with robbing a Winona, Minnesota, bank in June 2005, having been arrested nearby and identified by bank staff. The main evidence against him was his hold-up note, which began: "Hi, I'm Thomas Mason."

UNLUCKY CLOVER

Despite spending more than half his life in U.S. jails, George Kaminski has collected nearly 73,000 four-leaf clovers. He found all of them in the grounds of various Pennsylvania prisons, but when he was moved to a minimum-security facility in

MAD LEAP

A man was injured in 2005 when he jumped from a car traveling at 60 mph (96 km/h) in an effort to retrieve a cigarette that had blown out of the passenger-side window. Jeff Foran suffered trauma to his eyes, nose, and chin.

PARK PATROL

In an incredible feat of endurance, Christopher Calfee, a 38-year-old schoolteacher from Richmond, Virginia, ran around a park for nearly 92 hours in September 2005 without stopping for sleep. For four days and four nights he lapped Chesterfield's Pocahontas State Park. Apart from a three-hour halt to recover from the effects of dehydration, Calfee's only other breaks were for food at the end of each 25-mi (40-km) stint. But he never slept during the 316-mi (508-km) run. The pain was so intense that he had to protect his blistered toes with duct tape.

NIGHTTIME MOWER

Ian Armstrong, from Cheshire, England, got up to mow the lawn in the middle of the night while sleepwalking.

DRIVING BLIND

Stephen Hearn, from Birmingham, England, crashed his car at 70 mph (113 km/h) while sleepwalking near his home. When Stephen was found, he was in his pajamas and still snoring.

CORN LADY

In 1938, Virginia Winn, of Texas, stitched 60,000 grains of corn onto an evening dress, one by one. The gown weighed 40 lb (18 kg).

DOG TRAIN RIDE

When Archie the black labrador became separated from his owner at a Scottish railway station in 2005, he decided to take the train, not only choosing the right one, but also getting off at the correct station! When the Aberdeen to Inverness train pulled in to the station, Archie, having lost sight of his owner and perhaps fearing a long walk home, trotted aboard. The clever dog got off 12 minutes later at the next stop, Insch, his local station.

DELAYED REVENGE

In 1893, Texan Henry Ziegland jilted his girlfriend, as a result of which she killed herself. Bent on revenge, her brother shot Ziegland in the face, but the bullet only grazed him before lodging in a nearby tree. A full 20 years later, Ziegland was using dynamite to uproot that same tree when the explosion blasted the bullet from the trunk. The bullet struck Ziegland in the head, killing him.

BERMUDA TRIANGLE

While riding a moped in Bermuda in 1975, a man was killed by a taxi. A year later, his brother was killed riding the same moped after being hit by the same taxi, driven by the same driver. The taxi was even carrying the same passenger.

ELVIS RELICS

Among the many Elvis Presley relics that have sold on eBay are a branch from a tree ($900) and a hanging plastic fern ($750), both from his Graceland home, and a ball from his pool table ($1,800). However, a tooth said to be from Elvis's mouth failed to sell when no one bid the asking price of $100,000.

WAVE RIDER

Brazilian surfer Serginho Laus achieved a lifetime's ambition in June 2005 when he rode one continuous wave for 33 minutes, and a distance of 6.3 mi (10.1 km). He was able to ride the wave up the mouth of the Araguari River in northeast Brazil thanks to a "bore" created by a change in the tides.

UNDERWATER MAIL

The island nation of Vanuatu in the Pacific Ocean has opened the world's first underwater post office, which is manned by postal workers in diving gear!

SUPER SELLER

Bargain hunter Suzie Eads, of Rantoul, Kansas, has sold so many items on eBay that she has been able to build a house for her family with the proceeds. She has auctioned more than 17,000 items altogether, including a discarded beer can for $380. She even drives with the licence plate EBAY QUN.

CLIP CHAIN

Eisenhower Junior High School, in Taylorsville, Utah, is a school with a difference. The pupils have a habit of setting themselves amazing challenges. On March 26–27, 2004, the students created a "Mega Chain" that measured 22.17 mi (35.68 km) long and used 1,560,377 paper clips. They took 24 hours and divided the team into different roles to achieve this incredible feat.

MIND-BENDER

Magician Paul Carpenter, from Houston, Texas, performs the art of psycho-kinetics, or metal bending, wowing audiences across the U.S.

LIGHTNING CONDUCTOR

With Carl Mize, lightning doesn't just strike twice—it's struck four times already! In 2005, Mize was hit for the fourth time, while working on the University of Oklahoma campus. Mize was hospitalized for four days before being discharged.

BULLETPROOF CASE

British manufacturers have devised a special bulletproof briefcase. If the user is fired at, the brown leather case can be flipped open and used as a shield able to withstand handguns up to a .44 Magnum.

PUMPKIN PADDLERS

Howard Dill grows pumpkins partly for their seeds and partly for carving out for racing. He cultivates an oversized variety of pumpkin called Atlantic Giant, and after selling the seeds he donates the hollowed-out fruit for use in the famous annual pumpkin paddling regatta at Windsor, Nova Scotia, Canada. In the 2005 event, 40 competitors paddled their way across Lake Pesaquid while sitting in pumpkins that weighed more than 600 lb (272 kg). The winner usually

TRUNK ROAD

In 1934, a fallen redwood tree, which was about 2,000 years old, was converted into an auto highway in the Giant Forest, California.

manages to get round the course in about 10 minutes.

UNINVITED GUEST

When Beverly Mitchell returned to her home in Douglasville, Georgia, after a two-week holiday, she discovered that the lights were on and a strange car was parked in her driveway. Another woman, a stranger, had moved in, redecorated the rooms, and was even wearing Mitchell's own clothes.

FLYING NUN

Madonna Buder has definitely got the triathlon habit. As well as being a Canadian record-holder and Ironman legend, she leads a quieter life as a Roman Catholic nun. Now in her seventies, Sister Madonna, from Spokane, Washington, has completed well over 300 triathlons. She took up running in 1978. Before entering her first Boston marathon, she sought permission from the local Bishop to take part.

LIFTED CAR

Despite fracturing her spine and damaging two vertebrae in a car crash near Washington, England, Kyla Smith managed to lift the one-ton car—about 20 times her own weight—6 in (15 cm) off the ground in the attempt to free her trapped friend.

STING FOR YOUR SUPPER

A Chinese man not only catches wasps, he also eats them! Zhong Zhisheng, from Shaoguan City, does not charge people for removing wasps nests from their homes, on condition that he is allowed to take the insects home and fry them.

45

PACKED CHURCH

Canadian bride Christa Rasanayagam didn't exactly want her wedding in Ontario in 2004 to be a quiet affair. She was accompanied up the aisle by no fewer than 79 bridesmaids, aged from one to 79, who jostled for room with the groom's 47 best men.

BUMPY LANDING

A German driver who was using an airport runway to practice high-speed driving had a lucky escape in 2005 when a plane landed on his roof! The 55-year-old Porsche driver was traveling at more than 100 mph (160 km/h) near Bitburg when the bizarre collision occurred.

SHORT TERM

Believe it or not, there was a man who was president of the U.S. for just one day! When James K. Polk's term ended at noon on Sunday, March 4, 1849, and his successor, Zachary Taylor, refused to be sworn in until the following

HUMAN DART

Evgeny Kuznetsov, from Dzerzhinsk, Russia, set himself up as a human dartboard in Moscow in January 2006. Darts were hurled at his back— amazingly, without drawing a drop of blood.

YOUNG AT HEART

Although she is an impressive 96 years old, Peggy Barrett regularly takes to the skies in a glider. She and other 90-and-over pensioners from Gloucester, England, have formed the Gliding Nonagenarians.

day, David Rice Atchison, the president pro tem of the Senate, technically ruled the country in the intervening period. Asked what he did on that historic day, Rice admitted that he mostly slept after a succession of late nights.

NIAGARA PLUNGE

In October 2003, Kirk Jones, of Canton, Michigan, went over Niagara Falls without safety equipment and lived. Tourists saw Jones float by on his back in the swift Niagara River, plunge over the 180-ft (55-m) Horseshoe Falls on the Canadian side, then drag himself out of the water onto the rocks below.

PARACHUTE AHEAD

Parachutist Maria Ganelli, aged 40, had a fortunate escape in August 2005 when she landed in the middle of Italy's busy Adriatica Highway. She had planned to come down in a nearby field, but gusting winds pushed her off her chosen course and stunned drivers were forced to swerve to avoid hitting her.

ACKNOWLEDGMENTS

FRONT COVER (b/l) Jerilyn Tabor, Alison Slon, Doug Levere, (t/r) Scott Stewart; 4 (l) Jerilyn Tabor, Alison Slon, Doug Levere; 5 (r) Scott Stewart; 6-7 Jerilyn Tabor, Alison Slon, Doug Levere; 8 Chris Radburn/PA Archive/PA Photos; 9 Dougie Hendry/Rex Features; 11 Joe Jennings; 12-13 Reuters/Sukree Sukplang; 14 Reuters/China Daily Information Corp-CDIC; 15 Drahoslav Ramik/CTK/Camera Press; 16 Reuters/Ho New; 18-19 Troy Waters; 20 Sutton-Hibbert/Rex Features; 21 Noah Berger/AP/PA Photos; 22 Scott Stewart; 23 Ken "Spear" Flick and Steve Santini; 24-25 Andy Reed/Barcroft Media; 25 (t) DPA Deutsche Press-Agentur/DPA/PA Photos; 26 Steve Bunn; 27 Dick Jones; 28 Jessica Hill/AP/Press Association Images; 29 CP Canadian Press/Canada Press/PA Photos; 32-33 Reuters/Allistair Mitchell; 34 Ben Philips/Barcroft Media; 35 Reuters/David Bebber; 36 Feature China/Barcroft Media; 38-39 www.voltini.com; 40 Reuters/Gopal Chitrakar; 43 R. Clayton Brough and Eisenhower JHS; 44 Paul Carpenter; 46 Reuters; 47 Barry Batchelor/PA Archive/PA Photos

KEY t = top, b = bottom, c = center, l = left, r = right, sp = single page, dp = double page

All other photos are from Ripley's Entertainment Inc.
Every attempt has been made to acknowledge correctly and contact copyright holders and we apologize in advance for any unintentional errors or omissions, which will be corrected in future editions.